Don't Forget to Ge[t]

As my way of saying "thanks fo[r]
free gift for you.

"DASH Diet Desserts"

Visit the link below to download now.

www.GoodLivingPublishing.com/DASHchicken

Contents

DASH Diet 4
DASH Foods 6
Soup Recipes 8
    Asparagus Soup 9
    Curried Chicken & Carrot Soup 11
    Ginger Noodle Soup 13
    Chicken & Mushroom Soup 15
    Lemon Soup 17
    Spiced Chicken & Bean Soup 19
Salad Recipes 21
    Bean Salad in a Balsamic Dressing 22
    Tangy Orange Salad 23
    Blue Cheese Chicken Salad 25
    Pineapple Salad 26
    Couscous Salad 27
Main Course Recipes 28
    Chicken Piccata 29
    Chicken Cacciatore 31
    Beansprout Stir Fry 33
    Quesadillas 34
    Chicken in a Wild Tarragon Rice 36
    Balsamic Glazed Roast Dinner 37
    Chicken Chilli Con Carne 39
    Honey Glazed Chicken 41
    Whiskey Infused Mushroom Chicken 42
    Tomato & Basil Bake 44
    Chicken Wings in a Lime Mustard Sauce 45

Asian Spiced Chicken 47

Chorizo Stuffed Chicken 49

Quinoa Chicken & Veg 51

Simple Fajitas 53

Paella 55

Soft Shell Tacos 57

Mediterranean Inspired Chicken 59

Chicken & Vegetable Kabobs 60

Enjoy this book? 61

Other Books by Sarah Sophia 62

DASH Diet

What is the DASH Diet?

It is a dietary approach that was created by the National Heart, Lung and Blood Institute with the specific purpose of lowering blood pressure.

DASH is an acronym for Dietary Approaches to Stop Hypertension. In addition to lowering blood pressure, adopting the diet has been shown to protect the body against cancer, heart disease, diabetes, osteoporosis and strokes.

This dietary approach promotes health eating through a balanced diet with the main tenant being a low sodium consumption. Massively reducing, or eliminating, ones intake of sodium has shown great efficacy in the lowering of blood pressure.

In addition to the benefits mentioned above followers of the DASH diet also tend to lose a great amount of fat. As the DASH diet structures its food choices around whole grains, fruits, vegetables and lean proteins it is almost perfectly balanced to accelerate ones weight loss. Combine this with the elimination of manufactured and processed foods and it means that when following the DASH diet you are putting your body in fat loss heaven.

It would be wrong to just assume that the DASH diet is only for those wishing to lower blood pressure, it actually an excellent dietary approach for anyone looking to live a healthier life. The US government stated that the DASH Diet is an "exemplary way" for people of ages to eat.

In January 2014 it was rated by the US News and World Report as the best dietary approach available, it has now won this award 4 years in a row.

So, if you're looking for a new healthy approach to food then the DASH Diet may be perfect for you and your family.

DASH Foods

As mentioned in the previous chapter the DASH diet is a well-balanced approach to healthy eating that promotes eating wholefoods and the reduction of sodium.

You might be wondering what foods you are allowed to eat whilst on the DASH diet so I put together this chapter briefly outlining it for you.

You have probably guessed, given the title of this book, that chicken is allowed whilst following DASH, but what are the other foods?

- Whole Grains

- Fruit

- Vegetables, particularly green vegetables

- Dairy, but limit your intake

- Poultry

- Fish

- Lean beef, but try to limit to once or twice per week due to its high fat content

- Legumes and beans

- Nuts, but try to limit your intake to once or twice per week due to their high fat content

- Oils, use extra virgin olive oil if possible

As you can see the diet is very open and you should have no problems adopting it into your life. You won't need to cut out your favourite foods and, as this book will show, you can make amazingly delicious meals whilst following the DASH diet.

Just remember, when buying products always look for low-sodium/low-salt labelling.

Now you know a little more about the DASH Diet it's time to dive into the various chicken recipes I've put together for you. Every recipe in this book is perfect for those wanting to follow the DASH Diet and will help you lower your blood pressure, lose weight and generally be healthier.

Soup Recipes

Asparagus Soup

Makes 6 Servings.

Ingredients

2 chicken breasts, cut into thin strips

2 cups of potatoes, peeled and diced

½ lb. of asparagus, chopped

½ onion, chopped

2 stalks of celery, chopped

4 cups of water

2 tbsp of butter, unsalted

½ cup of whole-wheat flour

1 & ½ cups of fat-free milk

Lemon zest, to taste

Ground black pepper, to taste

Directions

Place a large pot over a high heat and add the chicken, potatoes, asparagus, onion, celery and water.

Bring to the boil then reduce the heat and cover. Let simmer for 20 minutes, stirring frequently.

Add the butter and stir it in before removing from the heat.

In a separate bowl whisk together the flour and the milk, add this slowly to the soup pot, stirring continually.

Put a high heat back on under the soup and cook for 5 minutes.

Take off the heat then season with pepper and lemon.

Curried Chicken & Carrot Soup

Makes 6 Servings.

Ingredients

2 cooked chicken breasts, chopped into small pieces

1 tbsp olive oil

1 tsp mustard seeds

½ onion, finely chopped

1 lb. of carrots, chopped into small pieces

1 tbsp ginger

½ jalapeno pepper, chopped

2 tsp curry powder

5 cups of chicken broth

¼ cup of chopped cilantro

2 tbsp lime juice

3 tbsp fat free plain yogurt

Grated lime zest

Directions

Place a pot over a medium heat and add the olive oil.

Add the mustard seeds and heat for 1 minute before adding the onion. Cook for 5 minutes stirring frequently.

Mix in the carrots, ginger, curry powder and jalapeno pepper. Cook for 2-3 minutes stirring frequently.

Pour in the stock, increase the heat to high and bring to the boil. Cover and reduce the heat to a simmer. Cook for 6 minutes.

Take off the heat and using a hand blender puree the soup for 8 minutes.

Turn the heat back to medium-low, add the remaining stock as well as the cooked chicken. Stir well and cook for 5 minutes.

Garnish with the cilantro, lime juice and yogurt.

Ginger Noodle Soup

Makes 6-8 Servings.

Ingredients

3 oz. of soba noodles

1 tbsp olive oil

1 onion, chopped

1 tbsp minced ginger

1 carrot, chopped

1 clove of garlic, minced

4 cups of chicken broth

2 tbsp reduced sodium soy sauce

3 chicken breasts, chopped

1 cup of soy milk

Directions

Place a filled with water pot over a medium heat and cook the noodles according to package instructions. Drain and set aside.

In the now empty pot heat the olive oil then add the onion. Cook for 5 minutes.

Stir in the ginger and carrot then cook for 2 minutes. Throw in the garlic and cook for 30 seconds, stirring frequently.

Pour in the stock, soy sauce and chicken. Bring everything to a boil before reducing the heat to low and simmering. Let cook for 8 minutes before mixing in the noodles.

Stir in the soy milk and cook for a further 4 minutes. Make sure you don't bring it to the boil as it will sour the milk.

Chicken & Mushroom Soup

Makes 4 Servings.

Ingredients

2 chicken breasts, sliced thinly

1 tbsp olive oil

½ onion, chopped

¼ cup of chopped celery

¼ cup of chopped carrots

1 & ½ of cups of sliced mushrooms

½ cup of white wine

2 & ½ cups of chicken broth

1 cup of fat free half & half

2 tbsp flour

¼ tsp dried thyme

Ground black pepper, to taste

1 cup of cooked wild rice

Directions

Place a pot over a medium heat and add the olive oil.

Once the oil is heated add the chicken and cook for 3 minutes, stirring frequently.

Add the celery, onion and carrots then cook for a further 3 minutes.

Pour in the chicken broth, the wine and the mushrooms. Cover and bring to the boil.

As the soup is coming to the boil mix together the half & half, the flour, the thyme and the pepper in a large bowl. Add the cooked rice to this and mix well.

When the soup is boiling turn the heat to low and add the rice mixture. Stir everything well and cook on low until the soup is thick.

Lemon Soup

Makes 4-5 Servings.

Ingredients

1 head of garlic, broken into cloves, skin removed

6 cups of chicken broth

½ cup of lemon juice

2 tbsp tarragon

Ground black pepper, to taste

2 chicken breasts, cut into small pieces

1 tbsp olive oil

Directions

Preheat your oven to 400F.

Line a baking tray with foil and place the garlic cloves on it. Cover the garlic with the foil and wrap it into a package.

Bake for 30 minutes in the oven then remove and set aside.

Place a large pot over a medium heat and add the oil along with the garlic cloves. Cook for 2 minutes and use the back of a spoon to flatten the garlic into a paste.

Add the chicken pieces and stir into the garlic paste. Cook for 4 minutes stirring frequently, add more oil if necessary.

Pour in the stock, the lemon juice and the tarragon, stir everything together. Season with black pepper and bring to the boil.

Once it is boiling reduce the heat to low and cover. Let simmer for 15 minutes.

Spiced Chicken & Bean Soup

Makes 4 Servings.

Ingredients

2 chicken breasts, cut into small chunks

2 tbsp olive oil

1 onion, chopped finely

1 tbsp garlic, minced

2 tbsp olive oil

1 can of cannellini beans

6 cups of chicken broth

Hot pepper flakes, to taste

½ head of escarole, thinly chopped

Ground black pepper, to taste

Directions

Preheat oven to 425F.

Lay foil on a baking tray and lay out the chicken pieces on it. Drizzle the oil over the top and place in oven until cooked through and well browned. Turn half way through cooking.

Remove chicken from the oven and let cool.

Take a large pot and place over a medium heat and add the olive oil.

Add the onions and sauté until translucent, usually this takes 3-4 minutes. Add the garlic and cook for further 1-2 minutes. Make sure they are well mixed.

Add the chicken stock, the beans, chicken chunks and pepper flakes.

Bring to the boil and then turn heat down and let it simmer for 30 minutes.

Whilst the soup is simmering away beautifully, chop your escarole. Add this to the soup and stir.

Cook for a further 20-30 minutes stirring occasionally. The escarole should start to break apart slightly and separate. If the soup begins to look too thick, add more stock.

Salad Recipes

Bean Salad in a Balsamic Dressing

Makes 4 Servings.

Ingredients

1 can of chickpeas, drained and rinsed

1 can of black beans, drained and rinsed

1 bag of mixed salad

2 chicken breasts, cooked and chopped into pieces

½ cup of balsamic vinegar

1 red onion, finely sliced

1 red bell pepper, sliced into thin strips

Ground black pepper, to taste

1 slice of well-done wholegrain toast, cut into small pieces

Directions

Add all ingredients, except the balsamic vinegar, to a large mixing bowl and gently toss.

Drizzle ½ of the balsamic in and toss again, make sure everything is well coated.

Separate onto different plates and then drizzle the remaining vinegar over everything.

Tangy Orange Salad

Makes 4 Servings.

Ingredients

½ cup of red wine vinegar

4 cloves of garlic, minced

1 tbsp olive oil

¼ cup of red onion, finely chopped

1 tbsp of celery, chopped

Ground black pepper, to taste

4 chicken breasts

2 cloves of garlic

1 bag of lettuce leaves

14 black olives, stoneless

2 oranges, peeled and sliced

Directions

Add the vinegar, celery, pepper, garlic, oil and onion to a bowl and mix together.

Place a pan over a medium heat and add more oil. As the oil heats take the whole garlic cloves and rub them over the chicken breasts. Discard the garlic.

Add to the pan and cook for 5 minutes per side, lower the heat and continue to cook until cooked through.

Remove from the pan, let rest on a chopping board for 4 minutes and then slice the breasts into thin strips.

In a large mixing bowl add the lettuce leaves, olives, half of the orange slices, toss everything well. Separate onto individual plates and serve the chicken strips atop the salad.

Drizzle the dressing over each serving and then top with the remaining orange slices.

Blue Cheese Chicken Salad

Makes 4 Servings.

Ingredients

2 cooked chicken breasts, cold and sliced into small pieces

4 tsp olive oil

2 tbsp balsamic vinegar

1 tbsp maple syrup

¼ tsp nutmeg

3 tsp of low-fat yogurt

1 large bag of spinach, roughly chopped

1 red onion, sliced

1 & ½ cups of sliced cucumber

1 & ½ cups of grape tomatoes

¼ cup of walnuts, chopped or crushed

¼ cup of blue cheese crumbled

Directions

Add the 3 tbsp of water, olive oil, vinegar, syrup, nutmeg and yogurt to a blender. Pulse well until smooth, this is going to be the dressing.

In a large mixing bowl add all the remaining ingredients and toss well.

Drizzle the dressing over the top, toss well and then serve.

Pineapple Salad

Makes 6 Servings.

Ingredients

4 chicken breasts, cut into chunks

1 tbsp olive oil

1 can of pineapple chunks, drained but reserve 3 tbsp of the juice

1 broccoli head cut into small florets

4 cups of baby spinach leaves

½ red onion, thinly sliced

¼ cup of olive oil

2 tbsp balsamic vinegar

2 tsp sugar

¼ tsp ground cinnamon

Directions

Place a pan over a medium heat and warm the olive oil.

Add the chicken to the pan and cook for 8-10 minutes. Stir frequently to ensure chicken is browned on all sides.

In a large bowl add the cooked chicken, pineapple, spinach, broccoli and onions. Mix everything together gently.

Next make the dressing by adding the pineapple juice, olive oil, vinegar, sugar and cinnamon to a bowl, whisk to combine.

Pour the dressing over the salad and toss well.

Couscous Salad

Makes 4 Servings.

Ingredients

1 cup of couscous

2 cooked chicken breasts, cold and chopped into small pieces

1 cup of zucchini, chopped into small pieces

1 red bell pepper, cut into small pieces

½ red onion, chopped

1 tsp ground cumin

½ tsp ground black pepper

½ cup reduced-fat Italian dressing

Directions

Cook the couscous according to the package instructions then let cool.

Transfer the couscous to a large mixing bowl then add all the other ingredients. Toss everything well.

Main Course Recipes

Chicken Piccata

Makes 4 Servings.

Ingredients

4 chicken breasts

½ cup of yellow cornmeal

1 tbsp lemon pepper seasoning

1 cup of Herb-ox instant broth

1 tbsp olive oil

2 tbsp lemon juice

2 tbsp of butter, unsalted

Directions

Pound the chicken breasts on a chopping board until flat and then set aside.

Place the broth over a medium heat and start to warm.

Mix the cornmeal and pepper seasoning together, spread out in large dish.

Dip the chicken breasts in the mix and coat in the seasoning. Use your hands to make sure the chicken breasts are well coated.

Place a deep pan over a medium-high heat and add the olive oil.

Once the oil is heated add the chicken breasts and cook for 4-5 minutes per side.

Remove the chicken from the pan and set aside. Pour the broth into the pan you cooked the chicken in, then add the lemon juice and butter. Reduce the heat to low until the butter is melted.

Return the chicken to the pan and cook for a further 4 minutes.

Serve over green vegetables.

Chicken Cacciatore

Makes 4 Servings.

Ingredients

4 chicken breasts

10 baby potatoes, sliced

1 can of chopped tomatoes

1 onion, roughly chopped

1 green bell pepper, cut into slices

1 tsp Italian herb seasoning

1 tbsp of olive oil

2 cloves of garlic, minced

1 15 oz. can of tomato sauce, no added salt

¼ tsp red pepper flakes or chilli flakes

Directions

Place a pan over a medium heat and add the olive oil.

Once the oil is heated add the garlic, onion and pepper. Cook for 5 minutes stirring frequently.

As this cooks mix together the tomatoes, tomato sauce, pepper flakes and herb seasoning in a large bowl.

Add the chicken to the pan and cook each side for 2 minutes.

Add the potato slices and cook for 1 minute.

Pour in the tomato mixture ensuring the chicken is covered. Reduce to a low heat so that everything is simmering.

Cover and let cook for 25-30 minutes.

Beansprout Stir Fry

Makes 4 Servings.

Ingredients

3 chicken breasts, sliced

2 carrots, sliced

1 onion, finely chopped

½ tsp ground ginger

1 bag of beansprouts

1 cup of chopped green beans

2 tbsp of olive oil

4 tbsp of soy sauce, low sodium

Directions

Place a wok or deep pan over a medium heat and add the olive oil.

Once the oil is heated add the chicken slices and cook for 3 minutes stirring frequently.

Add the carrots, onion, ginger and green beans. Cook for 3 minutes, stirring frequently.

Add the beansprouts and mix everything well.

Pour in the soy sauce, toss everything together and cook for 5 minutes.

Quesadillas

Makes 4 Servings.

Ingredients

2 chicken breasts, cut into small pieces

2 bell peppers, sliced into strips

1 red onion, thinly sliced

2 tsp olive oil

½ tsp ground cumin

½ tsp chili powder

2 tbsp chopped cilantro

1/3 cup of cream cheese

4 6" tortillas

1/3 cup of hot salsa

Directions

Preheat your oven to 425F.

Place a pan over a medium heat and add the olive oil.

Add the chicken, peppers and onion to the pan. Cook for 4 minutes, stirring frequently.

Sprinkle in the cilantro, cumin and chilli, mix well and then cook for a further 1 minute. Take off the heat and set the pan aside.

Lay out 2 of the tortillas on a baking tray and spread the cream cheese and salsa onto them. Spoon the chicken mixture evenly on top of these and then top each with the remaining tortillas.

Brush the top tortilla with olive oil and then transfer to the oven for 5 minutes.

Chicken in a Wild Tarragon Rice

Makes 4 Servings.

Ingredients

3 chicken breasts, sliced into thin strips

1 cup of chopped celery

1 red onion, finely chopped

1 tsp tarragon

2 cups of chicken broth

1 & ½ cups of dry white wine

¾ cup of uncooked rice

¾ cup of uncooked wild rice

Directions

Lay the rice in a baking dish and pour in 1 cup of the broth along with the wine to cover the rice. Set aside and let soak.

Preheat your oven to 300F.

Put a pan over a medium heat. Add the onion, celery, tarragon, chicken slices and the remaining broth. Cook for 10 minutes, stirring frequently.

Transfer the chicken and vegetables to the baking dish, spread out evenly. Cover with tin foil and place in the oven for 60 minutes.

Remember to check the dish after 30 minutes, if it is starting to dry out add more stock.

Balsamic Glazed Roast Dinner

Makes 6-8 Servings.

Ingredients

1 whole chicken

1 tsp dried rosemary

1 garlic clove, chopped

2 tbsp olive oil

Ground black pepper, to taste

6 sprigs of rosemary, chopped

½ cup of balsamic vinegar

1 tsp brown sugar

6 medium sized potatoes, chopped into wedges

4 carrots, chopped

1 onion, roughly chopped

Directions

Preheat your oven to 375F.

In a bowl mix together the rosemary and garlic, use the back of a spoon to mush it together.

Rub the chicken with the olive oil and then rub it with the garlic mixture. Place into an oven proof dish and set aside.

Put the potato wedges into a pot of hot water and bring to the boil. Cook for 5 minutes before draining.

Place the potatoes, onion, carrots and garlic pieces around the chicken, sprinkle with rosemary and then grind black pepper over everything. Cover the dish in foil.

Roast the chicken in the oven for 25 minutes per pound. Be sure to baste frequently with the juices from the dish. 10 minutes before finished cooking time remove the foil completely.

Set the chicken aside after cooking and recover with foil.

Place a small pot over a medium heat. Add the vinegar and sugar to the pan then cook until the sugar dissolves, ensure you are stirring frequently. The vinegar will be thickened at this point.

Serve the balsamic glaze over the chicken.

Chicken Chilli Con Carne

Makes 4 Servings.

Ingredients

1 lb. of ground chicken

1 onion, roughly chopped

1 can of chopped tomatoes

4 tbsp tomato paste

2 cans of kidney beans

1 cup of chopped celery

1 teaspoon sugar

2 tbsp chili powder

1 tbsp ground paprika or cayenne

1 tbsp olive oil

Directions

Place a large pot over a medium heat and add the olive oil.

Once the oil is warmed add the onion and cook for 4 minutes. Once the onion is cooked add the ground chicken and mix well. Brown the chicken for 8 minutes, stirring frequently.

Add the celery and cook for a further minute, make sure everything is well mixed.

Pour all the remaining ingredients, except the kidney beans, into the pot and mix well. Bring to a boil then turn the heat to low.

Add the kidney beans and mix in. Cover the pot and let simmer for 20 minutes.

Honey Glazed Chicken

Makes 4 Servings.

Ingredients

10 saltine crackers, crushed

2 tsp paprika

4 chicken breasts

6 tsp honey

1 large bag of mixed salad

1 tbsp of olive oil

Directions

Preheat your oven to 375F.

Grease a baking dish with the olive oil and set aside.

Add the crackers and paprika to a bowl, mix well.

In a different bowl toss the chicken breasts and honey together to coat well. Dip the chicken breasts into the cracker mix and evenly coat both sides. Lay the crusted chicken breasts in the baking dish.

Add to the oven and bake for 25 minutes.

Serve the chicken over the salad and use any remaining juices in the pan as dressing.

Whiskey Infused Mushroom Chicken

Makes 2 Servings.

Ingredients

2 chicken breasts

1 tsp of unsalted butter

3 cloves of garlic, minced or chopped

2 oz. shiitake mushrooms, chopped

2 oz. button mushrooms

¼ tsp thyme

¼ tsp rosemary

¼ cup whiskey

1 tbsp of olive oil

Directions

Place a pan over a medium heat and add the olive oil.

Once the oil is heated add the chicken breasts and cook for 4 minutes per side before lowering the heat.

Continue cooking on a low heat, turning frequently, until cooked fully through.

Whilst the chicken is cooking take a separate pan and add the butter. Once the butter begins to melt add the garlic, mushrooms, thyme and rosemary. Cook for 3 minutes and then remove from the heat.

Pour in the whiskey and mix well. Keep off the heat, but in the pan, until the chicken is cooked.

Once chicken is cooked pour the mushroom sauce over the top off the chicken and serve with mixed vegetables.

Tomato & Basil Bake

Makes 4 Servings.

Ingredients

2 large tomatoes, diced

2 tbsp chopped basil

1 tsp chopped oregano

1 tbsp minced garlic

1 tbsp olive oil

4 chicken breasts

8 cherry tomatoes

2 courgettes, chopped

Directions

Preheat your oven to 375F.

Add the diced tomatoes, basil, oregano and garlic to a bowl and mix well.

Grease a baking dish with the olive oil and then lay the chopped courgette on it, creating a base layer.

Lay the chicken breasts onto the courgette then spoon the tomato mixture over the chicken.

Add 4 tbsp of water and then place the cherry tomatoes around the dish.

Cover and bake in the oven for 25 minutes. 5 minutes before it finishes cooking remove the cover.

Chicken Wings in a Lime Mustard Sauce

Makes 4 Servings.

Ingredients

1 lb. of chicken wings

1 red onion, chopped

½ cup of fresh lime juice

2 tbsp capers

4 tbsp Dijon mustard

1 tsp hot sauce

3 cloves of garlic

1 cup of rice, uncooked

Directions

Preheat your oven to 375F.

Add the 3 tbsp of water, onion, lime juice, mustard, hot sauce and garlic to a blender. Pulse well.

Grease a baking tray and set aside.

Add the chicken wings to a large bowl along with the capers and mustard sauce from the blender. Use your hands to toss everything together.

Lay out the chicken wings on a baking tray and transfer it to the oven. Bake for 15 minutes before turning the wings and baking for another 15 minutes.

As the wings are baking, cook the rice as according to package instructions.

Serve the wings over the rice and use any juices to season the rice.

Asian Spiced Chicken

Makes 4 servings.

Ingredients

4 chicken breasts

2 tbsp sesame seeds

1 tsp ground coriander

⅛ tsp cayenne pepper

⅛ tsp celery seed

½ onion, finely chopped

¼ tsp ground cumin

⅛ tsp ground cinnamon

1 tbsp sesame oil

1 tbsp olive oil

2 blocks of noodles

1 tbsp of low sodium soy sauce

Directions

Preheat your oven to 400F.

Grease an oven proof dish with olive oil and set aside.

Place a pan over a medium heat and toast the sesame seeds for 2 minutes, be sure to stir frequently.

Remove from the heat and add the sesame oil, cinnamon, cumin, onion, celery seeds, cayenne and coriander. Mix everything together.

Place the chicken breasts in the baking dish and then rub with the spice mixture.

Bake in the oven for 25 minutes, or until the chicken is cooked through.

Whilst the chicken is in the oven cook the noodles according to package instructions. Drain the noodles and whilst in the sieve add the soy sauce and toss.

Serve the chicken over the noodles.

Chorizo Stuffed Chicken

Makes 2 Servings.

Ingredients

2 chicken breasts

2" of chorizo, chopped

2 cloves of garlic, minced

1 red onion, sliced finely

3 tbsp of goat's cheese

2 tbsp of olive oil

Ground black pepper, to taste

2 cups of spinach, pressed

1 head of broccoli, chopped into florets

Directions

Preheat your oven to 375F.

Slice lengthwise along the chicken breast creating a pocket within the breasts.

Stuff each chicken breast with the chorizo, garlic and goats cheese. Close the chicken breasts over to seal the ingredients inside.

Lay the onion out on an oven proof dish and then lay the chicken breasts on top. Drizzle everything with olive oil and bake in oven for 18-20 minutes.

As the chicken cooks, boil the broccoli and spinach then drain.

Add the broccoli and spinach to the oven proof dish. Season with pepper and then return to the oven for 5 minutes, or until chicken is fully cooked.

Quinoa Chicken & Veg

Makes 4 Servings

Ingredients

1 & ½ cups uncooked quinoa

2 cups chicken broth

4 tbsp of olive oil

2 cloves of garlic, minced

1 onion, finely chopped

2 chicken breasts, cut into thin strips

1 courgette, roughly chopped

1 large tomato, diced

80g feta cheese, crumbled into small pieces

6 basil leaves

½ a lime, squeezed

Directions

Pour the chicken stock into a pot and add the quinoa into it. Mix together and bring to the boil.

Reduce the heat to low and cover.

Let simmer for 15-20 minutes, or until the broth is fully absorbed. Fluff well with a fork then set aside.

Place a pan over a medium heat and add 2 tbsp of the olive oil. Heat the oil then add the onion and garlic, cook for 4 minutes.

Add the chicken then cook for 2 minutes, stir frequently.

Mix in the tomato and the courgette. Continue to cook, stirring frequently.

Once the chicken is cooked all the way through turn off the heat. Sprinkle in the cheese, basil and lime juice then mix well.

Serve over the quinoa.

Simple Fajitas

Makes 4 Servings.

Ingredients

4 chicken breasts, chopped into small pieces

2 bell peppers, cut into slices

1 onion, roughly chopped

3 tbsp olive oil

1 tsp ground paprika

1 tsp ground cayenne

2 cloves of garlic, minced

¼ cup of sour cream

½ cup of salsa

½ cup of cheddar cheese

1 lime

8 whole-wheat tortillas

Directions

Place a pan over a medium-high heat and add the olive oil.

Once the oil is heated add the vegetables, chicken and garlic. Cook for 5 minutes stirring frequently. Turn the heat to low then sprinkle in the paprika and cayenne. Cook for a further 2-3 minutes stirring frequently.

Sprinkle in the cheddar cheese, squeeze the lime in and then fold everything together. Continue to cook for 2 minutes.

When it comes to serving let people spoon their own chicken, salsa and sour cream onto their wraps.

Paella

Makes 4 Servings.

Ingredients

1 tsp olive oil

1 onion, sliced

2 leeks, thinly sliced

3 cloves of garlic, minced

4 chicken breasts, cut into chunks

2 large tomatoes, chopped

1 red bell pepper, sliced

½ cup of brown rice

1 tsp tarragon

2 cups of chicken broth

1 cup of frozen peas

¼ cup of chopped parsley

1 lemon, quartered

Directions

Place a pan over a medium heat and add the olive oil.

Mix in the leeks, onion, garlic and chicken. Cook for 5 minutes stirring frequently.

Add the tomatoes and the pepper, mix well and then cook for a further 4 minutes.

Sprinkle in the tarragon then add the rice. Mix everything well before adding the broth.

Bring to a boil over the medium heat then cover and switch the heat to low.

Let simmer for 8 minutes then fold in the frozen peas.

Let the paella simmer until the broth is fully absorbed, should be about 50 minutes. If it starts to dry out add more broth 4 tbsp at a time.

Once served garnish with a lemon wedge.

Soft Shell Tacos

Makes 4 Servings.

Ingredients

2 chicken breasts, cut into small pieces

1 tbsp olive oil

1 red onion, chopped

1 heaped cup of chopped zucchini

3 cloves of garlic, minced

4 medium tomatoes, diced

1 jalapeno chili, chopped

1 cup of frozen corn

1 cup of black beans

8 small corn tortillas

½ cup of smoked or hot salsa

Directions

Place a small pan over a medium heat and add the olive oil.

Once the oil is heated add the garlic, chicken and onion. Cook for 5 minutes stirring frequently.

Add the zucchini, tomatoes, chilli and black beans to the pan, mix everything together gently. Cook for 2 minutes, stirring occasionally.

Add the frozen corn and fold in. Turn the heat to low and cook for 2 minutes. Take off the heat and set aside.

Microwave the tortillas for 15 seconds.

To make the tacos just pile the filling onto the tortillas and top with salsa.

Mediterranean Inspired Chicken

Makes 2 Servings.

Ingredients

2 chicken breasts

4 tbsp sun dried tomatoes, chopped

2 tbsp black olives, stones removed and chopped

2 tsp minced garlic

2 tbsp pine nuts

2 tbsp balsamic vinegar

2 tbsp olive oil

Directions

Preheat your oven to 350F.

In a bowl toss together all ingredients except for the chicken breasts.

Slice the chicken along the side creating a pocket in the breast. Don't cut the whole way through.

Place the stuffing inside the chicken.

Lay on an oven proof dish, drizzle with more oil and bake for 15 minutes.

Serve with a side of steamed green vegetables.

Chicken & Vegetable Kabobs

Makes 2-3 Servings.

Ingredients

3 chicken breasts, chopped into large chunks

1 tbsp olive oil

Juice from half of a lemon

½ tsp thyme

2 shallots, peeled and halved

2 bell peppers, cut into thick chunks

6 cherry tomatoes

½ zucchini, cut into chunks

Ground black pepper, to taste

Skewers, soaked in water

Directions

In a bowl combine the oil, lemon juice, thyme, salt and pepper. Mix well and then add the chicken pieces to this mixture and coat well. Leave to sit in this marinade for 20 minutes.

Whilst you marinade the chicken preheat your broiler/grill.

Skewer the vegetables and chicken in an alternating fashion.

Season with pepper.

Place under grill and cook for about 5 minutes per side.

Enjoy this book?

Please leave a review and let others know what you liked about this book?

Reviews are so crucial to self-published authors like myself.

Even one quick sentence would mean the world to me!

Lots of Love

Sarah

Other Books by Sarah Sophia

Baking Gluten Free Bread: Simple Recipes for Busy Moms

Gluten Free Italian: Simple and Delicious Recipes for Cooking Italian Cuisine

The Hot Sauce Book: Recipes for Making Your Own Hot Sauces and Cooking With Them

Green Smoothie Delight: Delicious Smoothie and Juice Recipes to Burn Fat, Improve Your Health and Feel Awesome

The Quinoa Cookbook: Quick, Easy and Healthy Recipes Using Natures Superfood

The Budget Cookbook: Cook Restaurant Quality Meals at Home on a Shoestring Budget

All rights Reserved. No part of this publication or the information in it may be quoted from or reproduced in any form by means such as printing, scanning, photocopying or otherwise without prior written permission of the copyright holder.

Disclaimer and Terms of Use: Effort has been made to ensure that the information in this book is accurate and complete, however, the author and the publisher do not warrant the accuracy of the information, text and graphics contained within the book due to the rapidly changing nature of science, research, known and unknown facts and internet. The Author and the publisher do not hold any responsibility for errors, omissions or contrary interpretation of the subject matter herein. This book is presented solely for motivational and informational purposes only.

Printed in Great Britain
by Amazon